NEW YORK TEST PREP

Practice Test Book

Common Core Mathematics

Grade 4

ISBN 978-1503151789

CONTENTS

INTRODUCTION
For Parents, Teachers, and Tutors

About the New York Mathematics Tests

Students in New York will be assessed by taking the New York Common Core Mathematics Test. This practice test book will prepare students for this test. It contains two mini-tests to introduce students to the tests, and two full-length practice tests just like the real state tests.

Warming Up with the Mini-Tests

The mini-tests are short tests that will introduce students to the test and give them practice before taking the full-length practice tests. They include the types of questions students will encounter on the real tests, with a strong focus on more rigorous short-response and extended-response questions. The first two tests contains 10 questions each and the second two tests contain 20 questions each.

Taking the Practice Tests

The mini-tests are followed by two full-length practice tests. These have the same length, the same question types, and assess the same skills as the real tests. Just like the real tests, the practice tests are divided into three books. Students complete one book on three consecutive days. The content and time allowed for each book are summarized below.

Book	Questions	Expected Time	Time Allowed
1	25 multiple-choice questions	40 minutes	60 minutes
2	25 multiple-choice questions	40 minutes	60 minutes
3	6 short-response questions 4 extended-response questions	70 minutes	90 minutes

Calculators and Tools

Students should be provided with a ruler and a protractor to use on all parts of the test. Students are not allowed to use a calculator on any part of the Common Core tests, and so should complete all the practice tests without the use of a calculator.

Common Core Math Skills

All the questions on the New York Common Core Mathematics Test are based on the skills listed in the Common Core Learning Standards (CCLS). The answer key at the back of the book lists the specific skill covered by each question.

1   Which letter below has a line of symmetry?

J R W Z

Ⓐ J

Ⓑ R

Ⓒ W

Ⓓ Z

2   What kind of angle is each internal angle of the shape below?

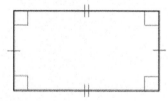

Ⓐ Acute

Ⓑ Right

Ⓒ Obtuse

Ⓓ Straight

3 Donna bought a lollipop for $0.60 and a candy for $0.15. How much change would Donna receive from $1?

    Ⓐ $0.15

    Ⓑ $0.25

    Ⓒ $0.35

    Ⓓ $0.75

4 Sandra started walking to school at 8:45 a.m. It took her 25 minutes to get to school. What time did she get to school?

    Ⓐ   9:00 a.m.

    Ⓑ   9:10 a.m.

    Ⓒ   9:15 a.m.

    Ⓓ   9:20 a.m.

5 The table below shows the shirt number of six players on a basketball team.

Player	Shirt Number
Jamie	27
Curtis	22
Wendell	31
Kevin	49

Which player has a prime number for a shirt number?

Ⓐ   Jamie

Ⓑ   Curtis

Ⓒ   Wendell

Ⓓ   Kevin

6 Which shaded model represents $\frac{5}{4}$?

Ⓐ

Ⓑ

Ⓒ

Ⓓ

7   The numbers below are arranged from least to greatest.

$$1,098 \quad 2,269 \quad \underline{\hspace{1.2cm}} \quad 2,350 \quad 2,699$$

Which numbers could go on the blank line?

Ⓐ   2,401

Ⓑ   2,320

Ⓒ   2,185

Ⓓ   2,239

8   Jenna buys 8 packets of letter paper. Each packet contains 12 sheets of paper. She uses 16 sheets of letter paper a week. How many weeks will it take her to use all the letter paper?

Show your work.

Answer _____ weeks

9   Kenneth got on a train at 9:30 in the morning. He got off the train at 1:20 in the afternoon. How long was Kenneth on the train for?

Show your work.

Answer _____ hours _____ minutes

10   A fish tank can hold 20 liters of water. How many milliliters of water can the fish tank hold?

Show your work.

Answer _____ ml

11 The table below shows the number of meals a café served on four different days.

Monday	Tuesday	Wednesday	Thursday
1,487	1,510	1,461	1,469

Place the numbers in order from the least to the most number of meals served.

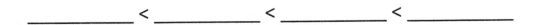

On Friday, the café served 200 more meals than on Tuesday. How many meals did the café serve on Friday?

_____

12 The table below shows the number of male and female students at Hill Street School.

Gender	Number
Male	2,629
Female	2,518

How many students go to the school in all?

Show your work.

Answer _____

How many more male students are there than female students?

Show your work.

Answer _____

13 A right triangle is shown below.

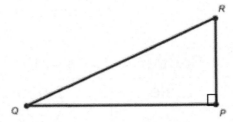

If angle *Q* measures 35°, what is the measure of angle *R*?

Show your work.

Answer _____°

14   The top of Kevin's dining room table is 4 feet long and 3 feet wide. Kevin wants to cover the middle of the table with tiles. He plans to leave a 6 inch border around the edge of the table and tile the center. Shade the area he will cover on the diagram below.

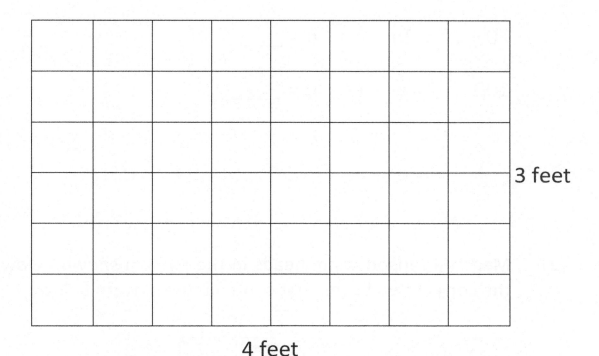

3 feet

4 feet

How many square feet of tiles will he need? Write your answer below.

_____ square feet

15 What value of *n* makes each number sentence below true? Write each value below.

35 + 3 = *n* + 5   *n* = _____

80 − 24 = 90 − *n*   *n* = _____

20 + 20 = 2*n*   *n* = _____

100 − 37 = *n* − 17   *n* = _____

16 Megan arranged some beads in the pattern shown below. Draw the correct two beads that continue the pattern below.

17 Which shaded model shows a fraction greater than $\frac{4}{5}$?

Ⓐ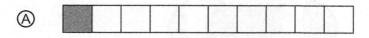

Ⓑ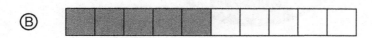

Ⓒ

Ⓓ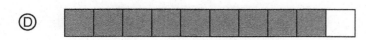

18 What is the number 457,869 rounded to the nearest ten thousand and the nearest thousand? Write your answers below.

Nearest ten thousand: _____

Nearest thousand: _____

19   Which is the best estimate of the length of a football?

    Ⓐ   10 inches

    Ⓑ   10 millimeters

    Ⓒ   10 meters

    Ⓓ   10 yards

20   Mia bought a milkshake. She was given the change shown below. How much change was Mia given? Write your answer below.

$ _____

END OF MINI-TEST 3

Common Core Mathematics

Mini-Test 4

Instructions

Read each question carefully. For each multiple-choice question, fill in the circle for the correct answer. For other types of questions, follow the directions given in the question.

You may use a ruler and a protractor to help you answer questions. You may not use a calculator on this test.

1   Which measurement is the best estimate of the length of a swimming pool?

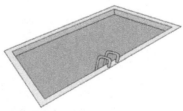

Ⓐ   10 millimeters

Ⓑ   10 centimeters

Ⓒ   10 kilometers

Ⓓ   10 meters

2   Circle **all** the angles of the shapes below that are obtuse.

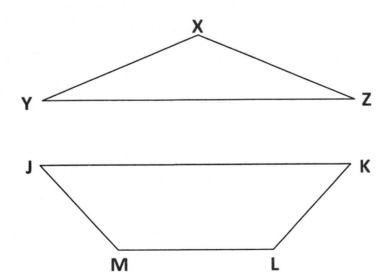

3   What part of the model is shaded?

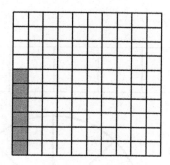

Ⓐ   6.0

Ⓑ   0.6

Ⓒ   0.06

Ⓓ   0.006

4   Which value of *p* makes the equation below true?

$$p \div 7 = 9$$

Ⓐ   49

Ⓑ   56

Ⓒ   63

Ⓓ   81

5 Shade the **two** diagrams below to represent fractions equivalent to $\frac{1}{2}$.

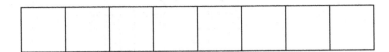

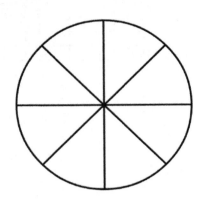

6 What is the rule to find the value of a term in the sequence below?

Position, *n*	Value of Term
1	3
2	6
3	9
4	12

Ⓐ $n \times 2$

Ⓑ $n \times 3$

Ⓒ $n + 2$

Ⓓ $n + 3$

7   Which statement below is true?

Ⓐ   386 > 389

Ⓑ   412 > 450

Ⓒ   611 < 610

Ⓓ   937 < 987

8   What is the sum of $\frac{1}{10}$ and $\frac{3}{100}$?

Show your work.

Answer _____

9   Mrs. Smyth has 82 colored pencils. She wants to divide them evenly between 8 people. How many whole pencils will each person receive?

Show your work.

Answer _____ pencils

10 The table below shows the number of students in each grade at the David Hall School.

Grade	Number of Students
3	254
4	235
5	229

How many students are there in all?

Show your work.

Answer _____

11 The diagram below represents the sum of $\frac{1}{4}$, $\frac{1}{4}$, and $\frac{1}{4}$. Shade the last grid to show the sum of $\frac{1}{4}$, $\frac{1}{4}$, and $\frac{1}{4}$.

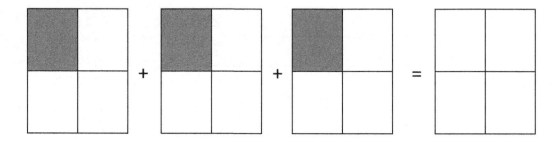

What is the sum of $\frac{1}{4}$, $\frac{1}{4}$, and $\frac{1}{4}$? Write your answer below.

_____

On the lines below, explain how the diagram helped you find the sum.

_____

_____

_____

_____

_____

12   What is the area of the square shown below? Be sure to include the correct units.

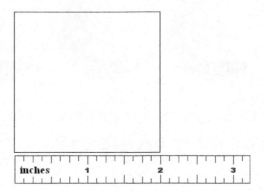

Show your work.

Answer _____

13   Jeremy had the coins shown below.

He swapped all the coins for nickels of the same total value. How many nickels should he have received?

Show your work.

Answer _____ nickels

14 A trapezoid is shown below. Circle **all** the acute angles of the trapezoid below.

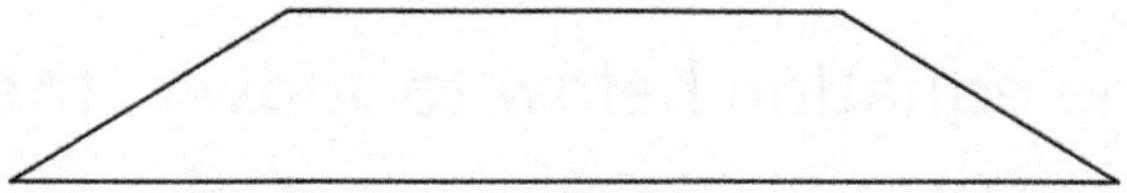

On the lines below, explain how you can determine whether the angles are acute without measuring them.

_____

_____

_____

_____

_____

15 The fine for having a DVD overdue is a basic fee of $4 plus an additional $2 for each day that the movie is overdue.

Complete the equation below to show *c*, the amount of the fine in dollars when a DVD is overdue for *d* days.

$$c = \underline{\hspace{1cm}} d + \underline{\hspace{1cm}}$$

Use the equation to find the cost of the fine when a DVD is overdue for 6 days. Write your answer below.

$\underline{\hspace{3cm}}$

16   The table below shows the total number of pieces of bread
Aaron used to make peanut butter and jelly sandwiches.

Number of Sandwiches	Number of Pieces of Bread
2	6
4	12
8	24

Which of these describes the relationship in the table?

Ⓐ   Number of sandwiches × 2 = number of pieces of bread

Ⓑ   Number of sandwiches × 3 = number of pieces of bread

Ⓒ   Number of sandwiches × 6 = number of pieces of bread

Ⓓ   Number of sandwiches × 8 = number of pieces of bread

17   Which unit would be best to use to measure the length of a box
of tissues?

Ⓐ   Yards

Ⓑ   Miles

Ⓒ   Centimeters

Ⓓ   Kilometers

18   Which number is a multiple of 8?

    Ⓐ   4

    Ⓑ   18

    Ⓒ   32

    Ⓓ   36

19   What is the sum of $1\frac{3}{4}$ and $\frac{1}{2}$? Complete the diagram below to help you find the answer.

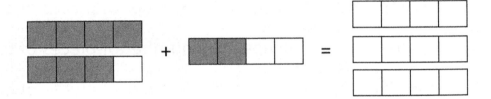

    Ⓐ   2

    Ⓑ $2\frac{1}{4}$

    Ⓒ $2\frac{1}{2}$

    Ⓓ $2\frac{3}{4}$

20 Patricia earns $9 per hour. In one week, she earned $360. How many hours did Patricia work that week?

Ⓐ 30 hours

Ⓑ 35 hours

Ⓒ 40 hours

Ⓓ 45 hours

END OF MINI-TEST 4

Common Core Mathematics

Practice Test 1

Book 1

Instructions

Read each question carefully. For each multiple-choice question, fill in the circle for the correct answer.

You may use a ruler and a protractor to help you answer questions. You may not use a calculator on this test.

---

1   What is the perimeter of the rectangle below?

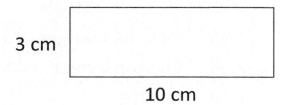

3 cm

10 cm

   Ⓐ   13 cm

   Ⓑ   30 cm

   Ⓒ   26 cm

   Ⓓ   60 cm

2   An array for the number 36 is shown below.

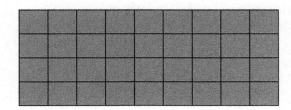

Which number is a factor of 36?

   Ⓐ   9

   Ⓑ   8

   Ⓒ   5

   Ⓓ   7

3   The table below shows the cost of food at a diner.

Drinks		Meals	
Small milkshake	$1.80	Plain hamburger	$3.50
Large milkshake	$2.00	Chicken burger	$4.20
Small soda	$1.10	Hotdog	$2.60
Large soda	$1.50	Meatball sub	$3.10
Fruit juice	$1.90	Quiche	$2.10

Lisa bought 2 items and spent exactly $4.00. Which two items could Lisa have bought?

Ⓐ   Meatball sub and a small soda

Ⓑ   Plain hamburger and a large soda

Ⓒ   Chicken burger and a small milkshake

Ⓓ   Quiche and a fruit juice

4 The table below shows the entry cost for a museum.

Adult	$10 per person
Child	$8 per person
Family (2 adults and 2 children)	$30 per family

How much would a family of 2 adults and 2 children save by buying a family ticket instead of individual tickets?

Ⓐ $2

Ⓑ $6

Ⓒ $8

Ⓓ $10

5 Maria is reading a book with 286 pages. She has read 38 pages. To the nearest ten, how many pages does Maria have left to read?

Ⓐ 240

Ⓑ 250

Ⓒ 260

Ⓓ 270

6 A box of beads contains 240 beads. Chang buys 4 boxes of beads. How many beads did Chang buy?

Ⓐ   860

Ⓑ   880

Ⓒ   960

Ⓓ   980

7   Liam has 6 pots he grows herbs in. He planted mint in $\frac{1}{4}$ of each pot. What fraction of a pot is the mint in total?

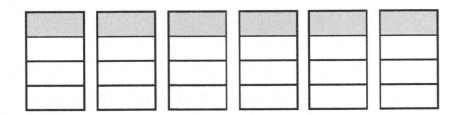

Ⓐ $1\frac{1}{2}$ pots

Ⓑ $1\frac{1}{4}$ pots

Ⓒ $1\frac{1}{6}$ pots

Ⓓ $1\frac{1}{8}$ pots

8   What is the measure of the angle shown below?

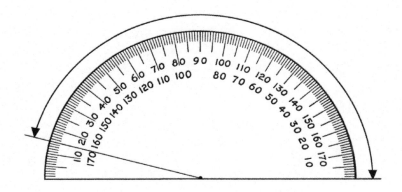

Ⓐ   15°

Ⓑ   25°

Ⓒ   165°

Ⓓ   175°

9   A pet shop sells fish for $3 each. The pet shop sold $96 worth of fish one day. How many fish did the pet shop sell that day?

Ⓐ   32

Ⓑ   36

Ⓒ   48

Ⓓ   288

10 Which number is a factor of 57?

    Ⓐ   11

    Ⓑ   13

    Ⓒ   17

    Ⓓ   19

11 Which number is a multiple of 6?

    Ⓐ   3

    Ⓑ   20

    Ⓒ   36

    Ⓓ   50

12 A motorbike has a weight of 255 kilograms. What is the weight of the motorbike in grams?

    Ⓐ   2,550 grams

    Ⓑ   25,500 grams

    Ⓒ   255,000 grams

    Ⓓ   2,550,000 grams

13 The fraction $\frac{56}{100}$ is plotted on the number line below. What decimal is plotted on the number line?

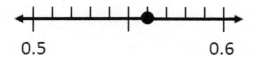

0.5   0.6

Ⓐ   5.6

Ⓑ   5.06

Ⓒ   0.56

Ⓓ   0.506

14 The table shows the relationship between feet and inches. How many feet would have a value of 72 inches?

Feet	Inches
1	12
2	24
3	36
	72

Ⓐ   4 feet

Ⓑ   6 feet

Ⓒ   8 feet

Ⓓ   12 feet

15 The angle that is formed between two lines has a measure of 95°. Which term describes this angle?

Ⓐ Acute

Ⓑ Right

Ⓒ Obtuse

Ⓓ Straight

16 Jayden wants to find the length of a paperclip. Which unit would Jayden be best to use?

Ⓐ Yards

Ⓑ Feet

Ⓒ Kilometers

Ⓓ Centimeters

17 There are 1,920 students at Jenna's school. Which of these is another way to write 1,920?

    Ⓐ   1,000 + 900 + 20

    Ⓑ   1,000 + 900 + 2

    Ⓒ   1,000 + 90 + 20

    Ⓓ   1,000 + 90 + 2

18 Which of the following describes the rule for this pattern?

1, 3, 6, 8, 11, 13, 16

    Ⓐ   Add 2, add 3

    Ⓑ   Add 2, multiply by 2

    Ⓒ   Multiply by 3, multiply by 2

    Ⓓ   Multiply by 3, add 3

19 Troy swapped 2 quarters for coins with the same value. Which of these could Troy have swapped his 2 quarters for?

   Ⓐ   25 pennies

   Ⓑ   10 dimes

   Ⓒ   4 nickels and 4 dimes

   Ⓓ   4 dimes and 10 pennies

20 Which number goes in the box to make the equation below true?

$$54 \div \boxed{} = 9$$

   Ⓐ   5

   Ⓑ   6

   Ⓒ   7

   Ⓓ   8

21   A pumpkin weighs 4 pounds. How many ounces does the pumpkin weigh?

Ⓐ   32 ounces

Ⓑ   40 ounces

Ⓒ   48 ounces

Ⓓ   64 ounces

22   The table below shows the population of 3 towns.

Town	Population
Franklin	18,725
Torine	24,214
Maxville	16,722

Which number sentence shows the best way to estimate how much greater the population of Torine is than Franklin?

Ⓐ   24,000 − 16,000 = 8,000

Ⓑ   24,000 − 17,000 = 7,000

Ⓒ   24,000 − 18,000 = 6,000

Ⓓ   24,000 − 19,000 = 5,000

23   A movie made $5,256,374 in its first weekend. What does the 2 in this number represent?

Ⓐ   Two thousand

Ⓑ   Twenty thousand

Ⓒ   Two hundred thousand

Ⓓ   Two million

24   Which shape below does **NOT** have a line of symmetry?

Ⓐ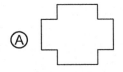

Ⓑ

Ⓒ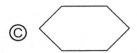

Ⓓ

25 The table shows the amount Davis spent on phone calls each month.

Month	Amount
April	$9.22
May	$9.09
June	$9.18
July	$9.05

In which month did Davis spend the least on phone calls?

Ⓐ April

Ⓑ May

Ⓒ June

Ⓓ July

END OF BOOK 1

Common Core Mathematics

Practice Test 1

Book 2

Instructions

Read each question carefully. For each multiple-choice question, fill in the circle for the correct answer.

You may use a ruler and a protractor to help you answer questions. You may not use a calculator on this test.

26   Emma listed factor pairs of the number 72, as shown below.

Factor Pairs for 72
1 and 72
36 and 2
24 and 3
12 and 6
9 and 8

Which of these should be added to the table?

Ⓐ   22 and 4

Ⓑ   14 and 7

Ⓒ   18 and 4

Ⓓ   15 and 7

27   The sizes of the drill bits in a set are measured in inches. Which size drill bit is greater than $\frac{1}{2}$ inch?

Ⓐ $\frac{3}{8}$ inch

Ⓑ $\frac{7}{16}$ inch

Ⓒ $\frac{1}{8}$ inch

Ⓓ $\frac{9}{16}$ inch

28   What is the rule to find the value of a term in the sequence below?

Position, n	Value of Term
1	3
2	4
3	5
4	6
5	7

Ⓐ $2n$

Ⓑ $3n$

Ⓒ $n + 2$

Ⓓ $n + 3$

29   A square garden has side lengths of 8 inches. What is the area of the garden?

Ⓐ   32 square inches

Ⓑ   36 square inches

Ⓒ   48 square inches

Ⓓ   64 square inches

30   Look at the line segments shown below.

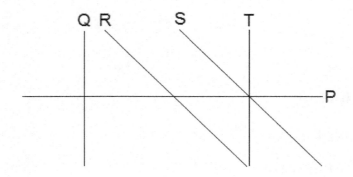

Which two line segments are parallel?

Ⓐ   Line segment P and line segment Q

Ⓑ   Line segment R and line segment S

Ⓒ   Line segment Q and line segment R

Ⓓ   Line segment S and line segment T

31 Which of these is the best estimate of the length of a baseball bat?

    Ⓐ   3 inches

    Ⓑ   3 feet

    Ⓒ   3 millimeters

    Ⓓ   3 centimeters

32 There are 40,260 people watching a baseball game. Which of these is another way to write 40,260?

    Ⓐ   4 + 2 + 6

    Ⓑ   40 + 2 + 60

    Ⓒ   40,000 + 200 + 6

    Ⓓ   40,000 + 200 + 60

33   The model below is shaded to show $2\frac{4}{10}$.

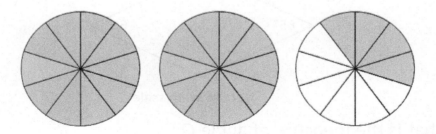

What decimal does the model represent?

Ⓐ   2.04

Ⓑ   2.4

Ⓒ   0.24

Ⓓ   20.4

34   Which of the following is another way to write the numeral 600,032?

Ⓐ   Six hundred thousand and thirty-two

Ⓑ   Six million and thirty-two

Ⓒ   Six hundred and thirty-two

Ⓓ   Six thousand and thirty-two

35   The drawing below shows a kite.

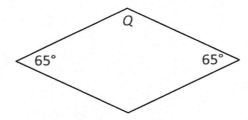

Not drawn to scale

What is the measure of angle *Q*?

Ⓐ   57.5°

Ⓑ   65°

Ⓒ   115°

Ⓓ   230°

36   Which number is a composite number?

Ⓐ   67

Ⓑ   73

Ⓒ   89

Ⓓ   91

37 What is 83,460 rounded to the nearest hundred?

Ⓐ   83,000

Ⓑ   84,000

Ⓒ   83,400

Ⓓ   83,500

38 Which pair of numbers completes the equation below?

$$\boxed{} \times 100 = \boxed{}$$

Ⓐ   60 and 6,000

Ⓑ   60 and 60,000

Ⓒ   6 and 60

Ⓓ   6 and 6,000

39 What is the measure of the angle shown below?

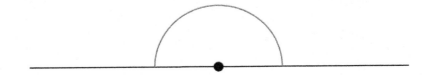

   Ⓐ   45°

   Ⓑ   90°

   Ⓒ   100°

   Ⓓ   180°

40 Kai found the coins shown below in the sofa. What is the value of the coins that Kai found?

   Ⓐ $1.26

   Ⓑ $1.36

   Ⓒ $1.45

   Ⓓ $2.36

41 Which figure below does **NOT** have any parallel sides?

Ⓐ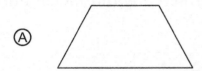

Ⓑ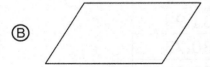

Ⓒ

Ⓓ

42 What is another way to write the fraction $\frac{9}{4}$?

Ⓐ $1\frac{1}{4}$

Ⓑ $1\frac{3}{4}$

Ⓒ $2\frac{1}{4}$

Ⓓ $2\frac{3}{4}$

43 Jackie made this table to show how much she received in tips on the four days that she worked. On which day did Jackie earn closest to $32?

Day	Amount
Monday	$32.55
Tuesday	$31.98
Thursday	$30.75
Friday	$32.09

Ⓐ   Monday

Ⓑ   Tuesday

Ⓒ   Thursday

Ⓓ   Friday

44 Bruce is counting his quarters. He puts them in 35 piles of 5. How could you work out the total value of the quarters?

Ⓐ   Divide 35 by 5, and multiply the result by $0.25

Ⓑ   Multiply 35 by 5, and multiply the result by $0.25

Ⓒ   Divide 35 by 5, and divide the result by $0.25

Ⓓ   Multiply 35 by 5, and divide the result by $0.25

45   A bakery makes muffins in batches of 12. The bakery made 18 batches of muffins. Which is the best estimate of the number of muffins made?

Ⓐ   100

Ⓑ   400

Ⓒ   250

Ⓓ   200

46   Katie saw the sign below at a fruit stand.

If Katie spent $6 on oranges, how many oranges would she get?

Ⓐ   10

Ⓑ   12

Ⓒ   20

Ⓓ   24

47 The normal price of a CD player is $298. During a sale, the CD player was $45 less than the normal price. What was the sale price of the CD player?

Ⓐ $343

Ⓑ $333

Ⓒ $263

Ⓓ $253

48 What is the product of 8 and 9?

Ⓐ 56

Ⓑ 64

Ⓒ 72

Ⓓ 81

49 Bagels are sold in packets of 4 or packets of 6. Kieran needs to buy exactly 32 bagels. Which set of packets could Kieran buy?

Ⓐ   2 packets of 4 bagels and 4 packets of 6 bagels

Ⓑ   3 packets of 4 bagels and 3 packets of 6 bagels

Ⓒ   4 packets of 4 bagels and 2 packets of 6 bagels

Ⓓ   5 packets of 4 bagels and 1 packet of 6 bagels

50 A bakery needs to order 60 eggs. There are 12 eggs in each carton. Which number sentence could be used to find c, the number of cartons the bakery should order?

Ⓐ $12 \times c = 60$

Ⓑ $12 \div c = 60$

Ⓒ $60 - 12 = c$

Ⓓ $60 \times 12 = c$

END OF BOOK 2

Common Core Mathematics

Practice Test 1

Book 3

Instructions

Read each question carefully. Then write your answer to the question. Be sure to show your work when the question asks you to.

You may use a ruler and a protractor to help you answer questions. You may not use a calculator on this test.

---

51   Joseph earns $8 per hour. In one week, he earned $280. How many hours did Joseph work that week? Write your answer below.

_____ hours

Joseph wants to earn $360 each week. How many hours will Joseph have to work to earn $360? Write your answer below.

_____ hours

Joseph decides to ask for a pay rise to $9 per hour. How many hours will Joseph have to work to earn $360 at $9 per hour? Write your answer below.

_____ hours

Joseph gets his pay rise to $9 per hour and works 30 hours. How much would Joseph make that week? Write your answer below.

$ _____

52   Shade the models below to show two fractions equivalent to $\frac{6}{10}$.

Then write the two fractions shaded on the lines below.

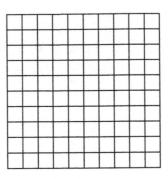

Fractions: _____ and _____

53 Plot the decimal 1.75 on the number line.

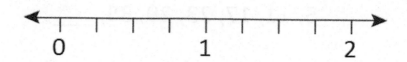

What fraction is equivalent to 1.75?

_____

54 Shade the model to show $1\frac{7}{10}$.

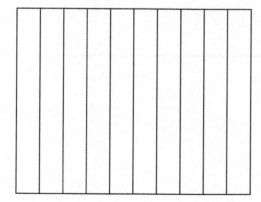 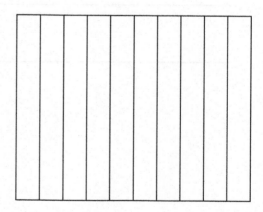

Write the mixed number $1\frac{7}{10}$ as an improper fraction.

_____

55   Look at the number pattern below.

$$5, 11, 17, 23, 29, 35, \underline{\quad}$$

If the pattern continues, which number will come next? Write your answer below.

_____

Will all the numbers in the pattern be odd numbers? Explain your answer.

_____

_____

_____

56   Salma drew these shapes.

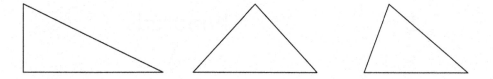

Identify the shape that has a line of symmetry. Draw the line of symmetry on the shape you identified.

On the lines below, describe how you can tell that the shape has a line of symmetry.

_____

_____

_____

_____

_____

57 Identify the place value for each digit in the number 234.15. Draw a line to match each digit with its place value.

1   hundreds

2   hundredths

3   ones

4   tens

5   tenths

Write the missing numbers on the lines to show 234.15 in expanded form.

($\underline{\hspace{1cm}}$ × 100) + ($\underline{\hspace{1cm}}$ × 10) + ($\underline{\hspace{1cm}}$ × 1) + ($\underline{\hspace{1cm}}$ × $\frac{1}{10}$) + ($\underline{\hspace{1cm}}$ × $\frac{1}{100}$)

58 A school divided its grade 4 students into 6 classes. There were exactly 26 students in each class. How many students were there in all?

Show your work.

Answer _____

59 A park has a length of 60 feet and a width of 40 feet. What is the area of the park?

Show your work.

Answer _____ square feet

60 Sort the figures below by placing the correct letters in each column of the table.

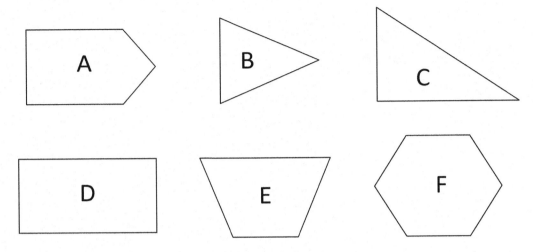

1 or more right angles	1 or more pairs of parallel sides	1 or more pairs of perpendicular sides

END OF BOOK 3

Common Core Mathematics

Practice Test 2

Book 1

Instructions

Read each question carefully. For each multiple-choice question, fill in the circle for the correct answer.

You may use a ruler and a protractor to help you answer questions. You may not use a calculator on this test.

---

1   Josephine boarded a train at 10:10 a.m. She got off the train at 12:55 p.m. How many minutes was she on the train for?

Ⓐ   105 minutes

Ⓑ   165 minutes

Ⓒ   205 minutes

Ⓓ   245 minutes

2   Ari is putting photos in an album. He can fit 6 photos on each page. He has 44 photos to place in the album. If he puts 6 photos on each page and the remainder on the last page, how many photos will be on the last page?

Ⓐ   1

Ⓑ   2

Ⓒ   3

Ⓓ   4

3   Which is a prime factor of the composite number 24?

Ⓐ   8

Ⓑ   7

Ⓒ   6

Ⓓ   3

4   Mia is setting up tables for a party. Each table can seat 6 people. Mia needs to seat 36 people. Mia wants to find how many tables she will need. Which equation could be solved to find the number of tables, t, that Mia needs?

Ⓐ $6 \times t = 36$

Ⓑ $6 \div t = 36$

Ⓒ $t + 6 = 36$

Ⓓ $t - 6 = 36$

5   Vienna bought a packet of 12 gift cards. She used 2 gift cards and her sister used 3 gift cards. What fraction of the gift cards did the two sisters use?

Ⓐ $\dfrac{1}{2}$

Ⓑ $\dfrac{2}{3}$

Ⓒ $\dfrac{5}{12}$

Ⓓ $\dfrac{1}{6}$

6   Zoe has 90 small lollipops, 30 large lollipops, and 55 candies. What is a common factor Zoe could use to divide the treats into equal groups?

Ⓐ   3

Ⓑ   5

Ⓒ   10

Ⓓ   15

7 A school cafeteria offered four Italian meal choices. The table below shows the number of meals served of each type.

Meal	Number Served
Pasta	151
Pizza	167
Salad	213
Risotto	117

Which is the best estimate of the total number of meals served?

Ⓐ   630

Ⓑ   650

Ⓒ   660

Ⓓ   670

8 Jay made 8 trays of 6 muffins each. He gave 12 muffins away. Which expression can be used to find how many muffins he had left?

Ⓐ $(8 \times 6) - 12$

Ⓑ $(8 \times 6) + 12$

Ⓒ $8 + 6 - 12$

Ⓓ $8 + 6 + 12$

9 Stevie had $1.45. She bought a drink for $1.20. Stevie was given one coin as change. Which coin should Stevie have been given?

Ⓐ A dime

Ⓑ A penny

Ⓒ A quarter

Ⓓ A nickel

10 Which of these is the best estimate of the mass of a watermelon?

Ⓐ 5 ounces

Ⓑ 5 grams

Ⓒ 5 pounds

Ⓓ 5 milligrams

11   The factor tree for the number 60 is shown below.

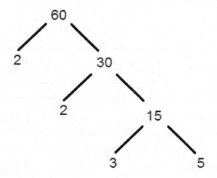

According to the factor tree, which statement is true?

Ⓐ   The number 30 is prime.

Ⓑ   The only prime factor of 60 is 2.

Ⓒ   The numbers 15 and 30 are prime factors of 60.

Ⓓ   The numbers 2, 3, and 5 are prime factors of 60.

12 Each number that was put into the number machine below changed according to a rule.

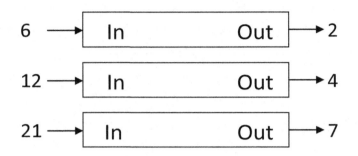

Which equation describes the rule for the number machine?

Ⓐ   Number in × 3 = number out

Ⓑ   Number in + 20 = number out

Ⓒ   Number in ÷ 3 = number out

Ⓓ   Number in − 8 = number out

13 Which digit is in the thousands place in the number 6,124,853?

Ⓐ   6

Ⓑ   1

Ⓒ   2

Ⓓ   4

14   Malcolm surveyed some people to find out how many pets they owned. The line plot shows the results of the survey.

Number of Pets

```
                    X
        X           X
        X           X
        X           X           X
        X           X           X           X           X
        X           X           X           X           X
      ――――――――――――――――――――――――――――――――――――――――――――――――――――
        0           1           2           3           4
```

How many people owned 2 or more pets?

Ⓐ   3

Ⓑ   4

Ⓒ   7

Ⓓ   9

15 The shaded model below represents a fraction.

Which model below represents an equivalent fraction?

Ⓐ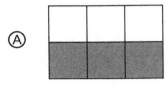

Ⓑ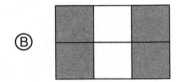

Ⓒ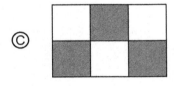

Ⓓ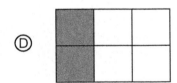

16 What decimal does the shaded model below represent?

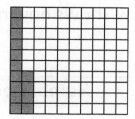

Ⓐ   1.4

Ⓑ   0.014

Ⓒ   0.14

Ⓓ   14.0

17 The diagram shows two sets of black and white stickers.

Which of these compares the portion of black stickers in each set?

Ⓐ $\dfrac{8}{9} > \dfrac{2}{3}$

Ⓑ $\dfrac{8}{9} < \dfrac{2}{9}$

Ⓒ $\dfrac{2}{3} < \dfrac{1}{3}$

Ⓓ $\dfrac{1}{9} > \dfrac{6}{9}$

18 The grade 4 students at Diane's school are collecting cans for a food drive. The table below shows how many cans each class collected.

Class	Number of Cans
Miss Adams	36
Mr. Walsh	28
Mrs. Naroda	47

Which is the best way to estimate the number of cans collected in all?

Ⓐ   30 + 20 + 40 = ?

Ⓑ   30 + 30 + 40 = ?

Ⓒ   40 + 30 + 50 = ?

Ⓓ   40 + 30 + 40 = ?

19 Which measurement is equal to 12 pints?

Ⓐ   3 quarts

Ⓑ   6 quarts

Ⓒ   24 quarts

Ⓓ   48 quarts

20 Which of these could be two of the angle measures of the right triangle below?

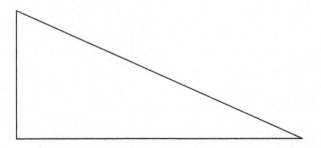

Ⓐ   20° and 60°

Ⓑ   25° and 65°

Ⓒ   30° and 70°

Ⓓ   45° and 75°

21 If *n* is a number in the pattern, which rule can be used to find the next number in the pattern?

4, 6, 8, 10, 12, 14, 16, ...

Ⓐ   *n* + 2

Ⓑ   *n* − 2

Ⓒ   *n* + 4

Ⓓ   *n* − 4

22 What part of the model is shaded?

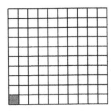

Ⓐ   0.01

Ⓑ   0.1

Ⓒ   1

Ⓓ   10

23 Which of these shapes has exactly one pair of perpendicular sides?

Ⓐ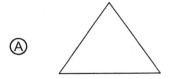

Ⓑ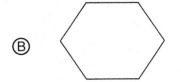

Ⓒ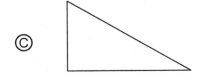

Ⓓ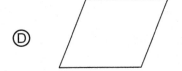

24 Which diagram shows a line of symmetry?

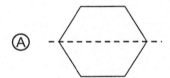

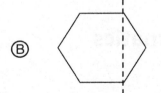

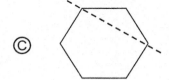

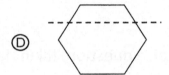

25 Thomas scored 5 times as many points in a basketball game as Jarrod. If Jarrod's number of points is represented as x, which of these shows Thomas's number of points?

Ⓐ $5 + x$

Ⓑ $5 - x$

Ⓒ $\dfrac{5}{x}$

Ⓓ $5x$

END OF BOOK 1

Common Core Mathematics

Practice Test 2

Book 2

Instructions

Read each question carefully. For each multiple-choice question, fill in the circle for the correct answer.

You may use a ruler and a protractor to help you answer questions. You may not use a calculator on this test.

---

26   Which of the following is a right triangle?

Ⓐ

Ⓑ

Ⓒ

Ⓓ

27   Madison used $1\frac{3}{4}$ cups of milk to make a milkshake. Which of the following is another way to write $1\frac{3}{4}$?

Ⓐ $\frac{1}{4} + \frac{3}{4}$

Ⓑ $\frac{4}{4} + \frac{3}{4}$

Ⓒ $\frac{1 \times 3}{4}$

Ⓓ $\frac{4 \times 3}{4}$

28 Andy was buying a used car. He had four cars in his price range to choose from. The four cars had the odometer readings listed below.

Car	Toyota	Ford	Honda	Saturn
Reading (miles)	22,482	21,987	23,689	22,501

If Andy decided to buy the car with the second highest odometer reading, which car would be buy?

Ⓐ Toyota

Ⓑ Ford

Ⓒ Honda

Ⓓ Saturn

29 Which number goes in the box to make the equation below true?

$$44 \div \boxed{} = 11$$

Ⓐ 4

Ⓑ 10

Ⓒ 11

Ⓓ 33

30 Which of the following has a mass of about 1 gram?

    Ⓐ A dictionary

    Ⓑ A pen

    Ⓒ A car

    Ⓓ A paper clip

31 Which model is shaded to show a fraction equivalent to $\frac{6}{10}$?

32 Jade made a pattern using marbles. The first four steps of the pattern are shown below.

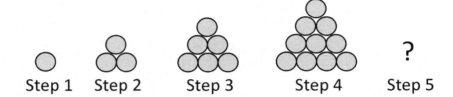

Step 1   Step 2   Step 3   Step 4   Step 5

If Jade continues the pattern, how many marbles will she need for Step 5?

Ⓐ   13

Ⓑ   14

Ⓒ   15

Ⓓ   16

33 A bookstore sold 40,905 books in May. Which of these is another way to write 40,905?

    Ⓐ   Four thousand nine hundred and five

    Ⓑ   Forty thousand ninety five

    Ⓒ   Four thousand ninety five

    Ⓓ   Forty thousand nine hundred and five

34 The thermometers below show the air temperature at 10 a.m. and 2 p.m. one day.

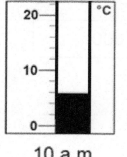 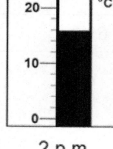

10 a.m.   2 p.m.

How much did the temperature rise by from 10 a.m. to 2 p.m.?

    Ⓐ   5°C

    Ⓑ   6°C

    Ⓒ   10°C

    Ⓓ   16°C

35 Which pair of numbers correctly completes this table?

Number	Number × 10
850	8,500
3,501	35,010
19	190

Ⓐ

28	208

Ⓑ

365	36,500

Ⓒ

1,987	19,870

Ⓓ

6	600

36 The model below shows $2\frac{8}{100}$ shaded.

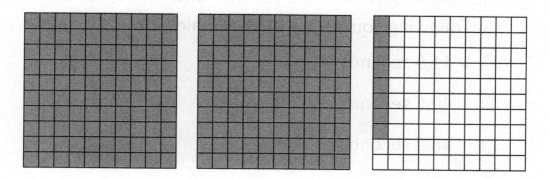

What decimal represents the shaded part of the model?

Ⓐ   2.8

Ⓑ   2.08

Ⓒ   200.8

Ⓓ   200.08

37 Joy started a hike at 1:50. It took Joy 2 hours and 25 minutes to finish the hike. What time did Joy finish the hike?

Ⓐ   3:35

Ⓑ   3:50

Ⓒ   4:05

Ⓓ   4:15

38 Ronald competed in a swimming race. All the students finished the race in between 42.5 seconds and 47.6 seconds. Which of the following could have been Ronald's time?

    Ⓐ   41.9 seconds

    Ⓑ   40.5 seconds

    Ⓒ   46.8 seconds

    Ⓓ   48.1 seconds

39 Which procedure can be used to find the next number in the sequence?

120, 60, 30, 15, …

    Ⓐ   Subtract 15 from the previous number

    Ⓑ   Add 15 to the previous number

    Ⓒ   Multiply the previous number by 2

    Ⓓ   Divide the previous number by 2

40 Which measurement below is the greatest?

    Ⓐ   2 kilometers

    Ⓑ   3,000 centimeters

    Ⓒ   2,500 meters

    Ⓓ   10,000 millimeters

41 Kevin is 1.45 meters tall. Brad is 20 centimeters taller than Kevin. What is Brad's height?

Ⓐ 1.452 meters

Ⓑ 1.47 meters

Ⓒ 1.65 meters

Ⓓ 21.45 meters

42 Camilla bought 4 bags of apples. Each bag weighed $\frac{3}{8}$ pounds. What was the total weight of the apples?

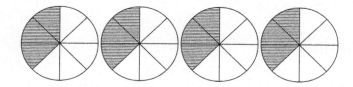

Ⓐ 3 pounds

Ⓑ $1\frac{1}{2}$ pounds

Ⓒ $1\frac{1}{8}$ pounds

Ⓓ $\frac{7}{8}$ pounds

43 Each number in Set P is related in the same way to the number beside it in Set Q.

Set P	Set Q
2	8
6	12
8	14
10	16

When given a number in Set P, what is one way to find its related number in Set Q?

Ⓐ Multiply by 4

Ⓑ Multiply by 2

Ⓒ Add 6

Ⓓ Add 8

44 In which of these does the number 8 make the equation true?

Ⓐ $48 \div \square = 6$

Ⓑ $\square \div 6 = 48$

Ⓒ $48 \times 6 = \square$

Ⓓ $\square \times 48 = 6$

45 There are 30,804 people living in Montville. Which of these is another way to write 30,804?

Ⓐ   30,000 + 800 + 4

Ⓑ   30 + 80 + 4

Ⓒ   3,000 + 800 + 40

Ⓓ   300 + 80 + 4

46 What does the circled area of the diagram show?

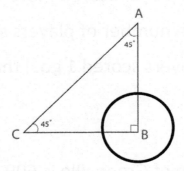

Ⓐ   A ray

Ⓑ   An angle

Ⓒ   A line segment

Ⓓ   A point

47 The line plot below shows how many goals each member of a soccer team scored in the season.

Soccer Goals

```
X       X
X       X       X
X       X       X       X
X       X       X       X       X
_____
0       1       2       3       4
```

Which statement is true?

Ⓐ Each player scored at least 1 goal.

Ⓑ Only one player scored more than 3 goals.

Ⓒ The same number of players scored 2 goals as scored 3 goals.

Ⓓ More players scored 1 goal than scored no goals.

48 The population of Greenville is 609,023. What does the 9 in this number represent?

Ⓐ Nine thousand

Ⓑ Ninety thousand

Ⓒ Nine hundred thousand

Ⓓ Ninety

49 Which is the best estimate of the angle between the hands of the clock?

Ⓐ   15°

Ⓑ   45°

Ⓒ   75°

Ⓓ   90°

50 It took Bianca 3 hours and 10 minutes to travel to her aunt's house. How long did the trip take in minutes?

Ⓐ   160 minutes

Ⓑ   180 minutes

Ⓒ   190 minutes

Ⓓ   310 minutes

END OF BOOK 2

Common Core Mathematics

Practice Test 2

Book 3

Instructions

Read each question carefully. Then write your answer to the question. Be sure to show your work when the question asks you to.

You may use a ruler and a protractor to help you answer questions. You may not use a calculator on this test.

---

51 Place the numbers listed below in order from lowest to highest.

35.061   35.101   35.077   35.009

Lowest   _____

_____

_____

Highest   _____

52 Which fraction and decimal is plotted on the number line below? Circle the **two** correct answers.

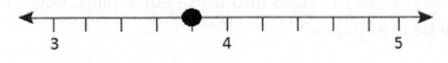

$3\frac{1}{4}$ $3\frac{1}{5}$ $3\frac{4}{5}$ $3\frac{3}{4}$ $3\frac{9}{10}$

3.4   3.5   3.75   3.8   3.9

53 Jed has 12 dimes, 18 nickels, and 24 pennies. He wants to divide them into as many piles as possible, but he wants the same number of dimes, nickels, and pennies in each pile.

Part A

What is the greatest number of equal piles Jed can divide the coins into?

Show your work.

Answer _____

Part B

If Jed divides the coins into those equal piles, how many pennies will be in each pile?

Show your work.

Answer _____

54   In the space below, sketch and label a right angle, an acute angle, and an obtuse angle.

Right Angle

Acute Angle

Obtuse Angle

Which angle sketched had to be an exact angle measure? Explain your answer.

_____

_____

_____

_____

55 Emma grouped the numbers from 10 to 20 into prime and composite numbers. Sort the numbers from 21 to 30 into prime and composite numbers. Write each number in the correct column of the table below.

Prime		Composite	
11	13	10	12
17	19	14	15
		16	18
		20	

Explain how the prime numbers are different from composite numbers.

_____

_____

_____

_____

56 A rectangular park has a length of 80 feet and a width of 40 feet.

Part A

What is the perimeter of the park in feet?

Show your work.

Answer _____ feet

Part B

What is the perimeter of the park in yards?

Show your work.

Answer _____ yards

57 Use the model below to find the sum of $\frac{3}{10}$ and $\frac{17}{100}$.

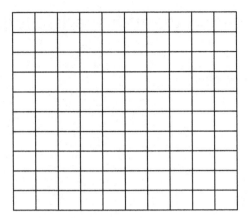

Answer _____

58 Ben answered $\frac{70}{100}$ of the questions on a test correctly. What decimal is equivalent to $\frac{70}{100}$?

Show your work.

Answer _____

59 Trevor's baby sister had a nap for $1\frac{3}{4}$ hours. How many minutes did she nap for?

Show your work.

Answer _____ minutes

60   Circle **all** the statements that correctly describe the rhombus below.

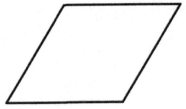

2 pairs of parallel sides

2 pairs of perpendicular sides

4 equal angles

4 right angles

4 congruent sides

Write the name of the shape that is described by **all** the statements above.

_____

END OF BOOK 3

ANSWER KEY

Common Core Learning Standards

The state of New York has adopted the Common Core Learning Standards. Student learning throughout the year is based on these standards, and all the questions on the state tests assess these standards. Just like the real state assessments, the questions in this book test whether students have the knowledge and skills described in the Common Core Learning Standards.

Assessing Skills and Knowledge

The skills listed in the Common Core Learning Standards are divided into five topics, or clusters. These are:

- Operations and Algebraic Thinking
- Number and Operations in Base Ten
- Number and Operations – Fractions
- Measurement and Data
- Geometry

The answer key identifies the topic for each question. Use the topics listed to identify general areas of strength and weakness. Then target revision and instruction accordingly.

The answer key also identifies the specific math skill that each question is testing. Use the skills listed to identify skills that the student is lacking. Then target revision and instruction accordingly.

Scoring Short-Response and Extended-Response Questions

This practice test book includes short-response and extended-response questions, where students provide a written answer to a question or complete a task. These questions are often scored based on the final answer given as well as the work shown. When asked to show work, students may show calculations, use diagrams, or explain their thinking or process in words. Any form of work that shows the student's understanding can be accepted. Other questions are scored based on tasks completed, explanations given, or justifications given. Answers are provided for these questions, as well as guidance on how to score the questions.

Common Core Mathematics, Mini-Test 1

Question	Answer	Topic	Common Core Learning Standard
1	B	Number & Operations-Fractions	Understand addition and subtraction of fractions as joining and separating parts referring to the same whole.
2	1st, 3rd, and 4th	Number & Operations-Fractions	Decompose a fraction into a sum of fractions with the same denominator in more than one way, recording each decomposition by an equation.
3	D	Number & Operations-Fractions	Compare two decimals to hundredths by reasoning about their size.
4	A	Operations/Algebraic Thinking	Determine whether a given whole number in the range 1–100 is prime or composite.
5	3rd and 5th	Number & Operations-Fractions	Compare two decimals to hundredths by reasoning about their size. Record the results of comparisons with the symbols >, =, or <.
6	See Below	Number & Operations in Base Ten	Multiply two two-digit numbers, using strategies based on place value and the properties of operations. Illustrate and explain the calculation by using equations, rectangular arrays, and/or area models.
7	6, 14, 22, 30, 38	Operations/Algebraic Thinking	Generate a number or shape pattern that follows a given rule.
8	See Below	Measurement & Data	Make a line plot to display a data set of measurements in fractions of a unit (1/2, 1/4, 1/8). Solve problems involving addition and subtraction of fractions by using information presented in line plots.
9	See Below	Number & Operations-Fractions	Solve word problems involving addition and subtraction of fractions referring to the same whole and having like denominators, e.g., by using visual fraction models and equations to represent the problem.
10	See Below	Measurement & Data	Use the four operations to solve word problems involving money, including problems involving simple fractions or decimals.

Q6.
The area model should be completed with the numbers 40, 320, and 16.
Answer: 1176

Scoring Information
Give a total score out of 2.
Give a score of 1 for a correct area model.
Give a score of 1 for the correct answer.

Q8.
The line plot should be completed as shown below.

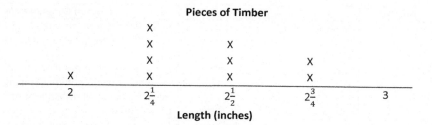

Answer: 9 inches

Scoring Information
Give a total score out of 3.
Give a score out of 2 for the line plot.
Give a score of 1 for the correct answer.

Q9.
The diagram should be shaded as shown below.

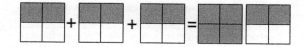

Improper fraction: $\frac{6}{4}$
Mixed number: $1\frac{1}{2}$

Scoring Information
Give a total score out of 3.
Give a score out of 1 for the shaded diagram.
Give a score of 1 for the correct improper fraction.
Give a score of 1 for the correct mixed number.

Q10.
$5.67
$6.33

Scoring Information
Give a total score out of 2.
Give a score of 1 for each correct answer.

Common Core Mathematics, Mini-Test 2

Question	Answer	Topic	Common Core Learning Standard
1	D	Measurement & Data	An angle that turns through 1/360 of a circle is called a "one-degree angle," and can be used to measure angles. Recognize angle measure as additive. When an angle is decomposed into non-overlapping parts, the angle measure of the whole is the sum of the angle measures of the parts.
2	1st, 2nd, 4th, and 5th	Number & Operations-Fractions	Understand addition and subtraction of fractions as joining and separating parts referring to the same whole.
3	A	Geometry	Classify two-dimensional figures based on the presence or absence of parallel or perpendicular lines, or the presence or absence of angles of a specified size.
4	B	Operations/Algebraic Thinking	Multiply or divide to solve word problems involving multiplicative comparison.
5	C	Measurement & Data	Use the four operations to solve word problems involving distances, including problems that require expressing measurements given in a larger unit in terms of a smaller unit.
6	22 tables	Number & Operations in Base Ten	Find whole-number quotients using strategies based on place value, the properties of operations, and/or the relationship between multiplication and division.
7	See Below	Measurement & Data	Recognize angle measure as additive. When an angle is decomposed into non-overlapping parts, the angle measure of the whole is the sum of the angle measures of the parts.
8	See Below	Measurement & Data	Represent and interpret data.
9	See Below	Number & Operations-Fractions	Explain why a fraction a/b is equivalent to a fraction $(n \times a)/(n \times b)$ by using visual fraction models, with attention to how the number and size of the parts differ even though the two fractions themselves are the same size. Use this principle to recognize and generate equivalent fractions.
10	See Below	Measurement & Data	Apply the area and perimeter formulas for rectangles in real world and mathematical problems.

Q7.
The straight angle should be divided into four angles of 45° each, as shown below.

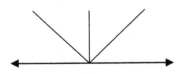

Answer: 45°
The term "acute" should be circled.

Scoring Information
Give a total score out of 3.
Give a score of 1 for dividing the straight angle correctly.
Give a score of 1 for the correct angle measure.
Give a score of 1 for circling "acute."

Q8.
The student should complete the chart as shown below.

Student Votes for Field Trip Location

Museum	✓ ✓ ✓ ✓
Cinema	✓ ✓ ✓ ✓ ✓ ✓
Zoo	✓ ✓ ✓ ✓ ✓ ✓ ✓ ✓ ✓
Town Hall	✓ ✓ ✓

✓ = 4 votes

Answer: Cinema and Town Hall

Scoring Information
Give a total score out of 3.
Give a score out of 2 for the completed picture graph.
Give a score of 1 for the correct answer.

Q9.
The student should divide each rectangle into 8 equal rectangles. The possible ways of dividing the paper are shown below.

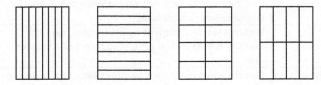

The student should explain that each piece of paper has the same area because they are all $\frac{1}{8}$ the size of the original piece of paper.

Scoring Information
Give a total score out of 3.
Give a score of 1 for each rectangle correctly divided.
Give a score out of 1 for the explanation.

Q10.
The student should add the missing dimensions 2 ft and 11 ft.
36 feet
37 tiles

Scoring Information
Give a total score out of 3.
Give a score of 0.5 for each correct dimension.
Give a score of 1 for each correct answer.

Common Core Mathematics, Mini-Test 3

Question	Answer	Topic	Common Core Learning Standard
1	C	Geometry	Identify line-symmetric figures and draw lines of symmetry.
2	B	Geometry	Draw points, lines, line segments, rays, angles (right, acute, obtuse), and perpendicular and parallel lines. Identify these in two-dimensional figures.
3	B	Measurement & Data	Use the four operations to solve word problems involving money.
4	B	Measurement & Data	Use the four operations to solve word problems involving intervals of time.
5	C	Operations/Algebraic Thinking	Determine whether a given whole number in the range 1–100 is prime or composite.
6	C	Number & Operations-Fractions	Decompose a fraction into a sum of fractions with the same denominator in more than one way, recording each decomposition by an equation. Justify decompositions, e.g., by using a visual fraction model.
7	B	Number & Operations in Base Ten	Compare two multi-digit numbers based on meanings of the digits in each place.
8	See Below	Operations/Algebraic Thinking	Solve multistep word problems posed with whole numbers and having whole-number answers using the four operations.
9	See Below	Measurement & Data	Use the four operations to solve word problems involving intervals of time.
10	See Below	Measurement & Data	Within a single system of measurement, express measurements in a larger unit in terms of a smaller unit.
11	See Below	Number & Operations in Base Ten	Compare two multi-digit numbers based on meanings of the digits in each place, using >, =, and < symbols to record the results of comparisons.
12	See Below	Number & Operations in Base Ten	Fluently add and subtract multi-digit whole numbers using the standard algorithm.
13	See Below	Measurement & Data	Solve addition and subtraction problems to find unknown angles on a diagram in real world and mathematical problems.
14	See Below	Measurement & Data	Use the four operations to solve word problems involving distances. Apply the area and perimeter formulas for rectangles in real world and mathematical problems.
15	33, 34, 20, 80	Operations/Algebraic Thinking	Represent problems using equations with a letter standing for the unknown quantity. Assess the reasonableness of answers using mental computation and estimation strategies including rounding.
16	oval, rectangle	Operations/Algebraic Thinking	Generate a number or shape pattern that follows a given rule.
17	D	Number & Operations-Fractions	Compare two fractions with different numerators and different denominators. Justify the conclusions, e.g., by using a visual fraction model.
18	460,000 458,000	Number & Operations in Base Ten	Use place value understanding to round multi-digit whole numbers to any place.
19	A	Measurement & Data	Know relative sizes of measurement units within one system of units.
20	$0.76	Measurement & Data	Use the four operations to solve word problems involving money.

Q8.
6 weeks

The work should show the calculation of 8 × 12 = 96 and 96 ÷ 16 = 6.

Scoring Information
Give a total score out of 2.
Give a score of 1 for the correct answer.
Give a score out of 1 for the working.

Q9.
3 hours 50 minutes

The student may find the time from 9:30 to midday and then add the time from midday to 1:20, find the hours from 9:30 to 12:30 and then add the minutes from 12:30 to 1:20, find the hours from 9:30 to 1:30 and then subtract 10 minutes, or find the minutes from 9:30 to 1:20 and then convert the time to hours and minutes.

Scoring Information
Give a total score out of 2.
Give a score of 1 for the correct answer.
Give a score out of 1 for the working.

Q10.
20,000 ml

The work should show an understanding that there are 1,000 milliliters in a liter, and show the calculation of 20 × 1,000 = 20,000.

Scoring Information
Give a total score out of 2.
Give a score of 1 for the correct answer.
Give a score out of 1 for the working.

Q11.
1,461 < 1,469 < 1,487 < 1,510
Answer: 1,710

Scoring Information
Give a total score out of 3.
Give a score of 0.5 for each number correctly ordered.
Give a score of 1 for the correct answer.

Q12.
5,147

The work should show the calculation of 2,629 + 2,518 = 5,147.

111

The work should show the calculation of 2,629 − 2,518 = 111.

Scoring Information
Give a total score out of 2.
Give a score of 1 for each correct answer.

Q13.
55°

The work should show an understanding that there are 180° in a triangle and subtract 90° and 35° from 180° to give the missing angle measure of 55°.

Scoring Information
Give a total score out of 2.
Give a score of 1 for the correct answer.
Give a score out of 1 for the working.

Q14.
The diagram should be shaded as below.

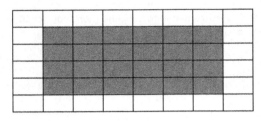

Answer: 6 square feet

Scoring Information
Give a total score out of 2.
Give a score of 1 for the correct shading.
Give a score of 1 for the correct answer.

Common Core Mathematics, Mini-Test 4

Question	Answer	Topic	Common Core Learning Standard
1	D	Measurement & Data	Know relative sizes of measurement units within one system of units.
2	X, M, L	Geometry	Draw points, lines, line segments, rays, angles (right, acute, obtuse), and perpendicular and parallel lines. Identify these in two-dimensional figures.
3	C	Number & Operations-Fractions	Use decimal notation for fractions with denominators 10 or 100.
4	C	Number & Operations in Base Ten	Find whole-number quotients using strategies based on place value, the properties of operations, and/or the relationship between multiplication and division.
5	Any 4 segments shaded	Number & Operations-Fractions	Explain why a fraction is equivalent to a fraction by using visual fraction models.
6	B	Operations/Algebraic Thinking	Generate and analyze patterns.
7	D	Number & Operations in Base Ten	Compare two multi-digit numbers based on meanings of the digits in each place, using >, =, and < symbols to record the results of comparisons.
8	See Below	Number & Operations-Fractions	Express a fraction with denominator 10 as an equivalent fraction with denominator 100, and use this technique to add two fractions with respective denominators 10 and 100.
9	See Below	Operations/Algebraic Thinking	Solve multistep word problems posed with whole numbers and having whole-number answers using the four operations, including problems in which remainders must be interpreted.
10	See Below	Number & Operations in Base Ten	Fluently add and subtract multi-digit whole numbers using the standard algorithm.
11	See Below	Number & Operations-Fractions	Decompose a fraction into a sum of fractions with the same denominator in more than one way, recording each decomposition by an equation. Justify decompositions, e.g., by using a visual fraction model.
12	See Below	Measurement & Data	Apply the area and perimeter formulas for rectangles in real world and mathematical problems.
13	See Below	Measurement & Data	Use the four operations to solve word problems involving money.
14	See Below	Geometry	Draw points, lines, line segments, rays, angles (right, acute, obtuse), and perpendicular and parallel lines. Identify these in two-dimensional figures.
15	See Below	Operations/Algebraic Thinking	Solve multistep word problems posed with whole numbers and having whole-number answers using the four operations, including problems in which remainders must be interpreted. Represent these problems using equations with a letter standing for the unknown quantity.
16	B	Operations/Algebraic Thinking	Generate and analyze patterns.
17	C	Measurement & Data	Know relative sizes of measurement units within one system of units.
18	C	Operations/Algebraic Thinking	Determine whether a given whole number in the range 1–100 is a multiple of a given one-digit number.
19	B	Number & Operations-Fractions	Understand addition and subtraction of fractions as joining and separating parts referring to the same whole.
20	C	Operations/Algebraic Thinking	Multiply or divide to solve word problems involving multiplicative comparison.

Q8.

$\dfrac{13}{100}$

The work should show converting $\frac{1}{10}$ to $\frac{10}{100}$, and then adding and $\frac{10}{100}$ and $\frac{3}{100}$.

Scoring Information
Give a total score out of 2.
Give a score of 1 for the correct answer.
Give a score out of 1 for the working.

Q9.
10 pencils

The work should show the calculation of 82 ÷ 8 = 10 remainder 2.

Scoring Information
Give a total score out of 2.
Give a score of 1 for the correct answer.
Give a score out of 1 for the working.

Q10.
718

The work should show the calculation of 254 + 235 + 229 = 718.

Scoring Information
Give a total score out of 2.
Give a score of 1 for the correct answer.
Give a score out of 1 for the working.

Q11.
The last grid of the model should have 3 of the 4 parts shaded.
Answer: $\frac{3}{4}$
The explanation should refer to the diagram showing that 3 of the 4 parts of the whole are shaded.

Scoring Information
Give a total score out of 3.
Give a score of 1 for the correct shading.
Give a score of 1 for the correct answer.
Give a score out of 1 for the explanation.

Q12.
4 square inches or 4 in^2

The work should show the side length as 2 inches, and show the calculation of 2 inches × 2 inches = 4 square inches.

Scoring Information
Give a total score out of 2.
Give a score of 1 for the correct numerical answer of 4.
Give a score of 1 for the correct units of square inches or in^2.

Q13.
15 nickels

The work may show that each quarter is equal to 25 cents, or 5 nickels, and then show 5 × 3 = 15. The work may also show that the quarters are equal to 75 cents, and a nickel is equal to 5 cents, and then show the calculation 75 ÷ 5 = 15.

Scoring Information
Give a total score out of 2.
Give a score of 1 for the correct answer.
Give a score out of 1 for the working.

Q14.
The two smallest angles should be circled.
The explanation should refer to how you can tell that the angles are less than a right angle.

Scoring Information
Give a total score out of 3.
Give a score of 1 for each correct angle circled.
Give a score out of 1 for the explanation.

Q15.
$c = 2d + 4$
Answer: $16

Scoring Information
Give a total score out of 3.
Give a score of 1 for the correct equation.
Give a score of 1 for the correct answer.
Give a score of 1 for using the correct value of $d = 6$.

Common Core Mathematics, Practice Test 1, Book 1

Question	Answer	Topic	Common Core Learning Standard
1	C	Measurement & Data	Apply the area and perimeter formulas for rectangles in real world and mathematical problems.
2	A	Operations/Algebraic Thinking	Recognize that a whole number is a multiple of each of its factors.
3	D	Measurement & Data	Use the four operations to solve word problems involving money.
4	B	Operations/Algebraic Thinking	Solve multistep word problems posed with whole numbers and having whole-number answers using the four operations.
5	B	Operations/Algebraic Thinking	Assess the reasonableness of answers using mental computation and estimation strategies including rounding.
6	C	Number & Operations in Base Ten	Multiply a whole number of up to four digits by a one-digit whole number using strategies based on place value and the properties of operations.
7	A	Number & Operations-Fractions	Apply and extend previous understandings of multiplication to multiply a fraction by a whole number.
8	C	Measurement & Data	Measure angles in whole-number degrees using a protractor.
9	A	Number & Operations in Base Ten	Find whole-number quotients and remainders with up to four-digit dividends and one-digit divisors.
10	D	Operations/Algebraic Thinking	Find all factor pairs for a whole number in the range 1–100.
11	C	Operations/Algebraic Thinking	Determine whether a given whole number in the range 1–100 is a multiple of a given one-digit number.
12	C	Measurement & Data	Within a single system of measurement, express measurements in a larger unit in terms of a smaller unit.
13	C	Number & Operations-Fractions	Use decimal notation for fractions with denominators 10 or 100.
14	B	Measurement & Data	Record measurement equivalents in a two-column table.
15	C	Geometry	Draw and identify right, acute, and obtuse angles.
16	D	Measurement & Data	Know relative sizes of measurement units within one system of units.
17	A	Number & Operations in Base Ten	Read and write multi-digit whole numbers using base-ten numerals, number names, and expanded form.
18	A	Operations/Algebraic Thinking	Generate and analyze patterns.
19	D	Measurement & Data	Use the four operations to solve word problems involving money.
20	B	Number & Operations in Base Ten	Find whole-number quotients using strategies based on place value, the properties of operations, and/or the relationship between multiplication and division.
21	D	Measurement & Data	Within a single system of measurement, express measurements in a larger unit in terms of a smaller unit.
22	D	Operations/Algebraic Thinking	Assess the reasonableness of answers using mental computation and estimation strategies including rounding.

23	C	Number & Operations in Base Ten	Recognize that in a multi-digit whole number, a digit in one place represents ten times what it represents in the place to its right.
24	B	Geometry	Identify line-symmetric figures and draw lines of symmetry.
25	D	Number & Operations-Fractions	Compare two decimals to hundredths by reasoning about their size.

Common Core Mathematics, Practice Test 1, Book 2

Question	Answer	Topic	Common Core Learning Standard
26	C	Operations/Algebraic Thinking	Find all factor pairs for a whole number in the range 1-100.
27	D	Number & Operations-Fractions	Compare two fractions with different numerators and different denominators.
28	C	Operations/Algebraic Thinking	Generate and analyze patterns.
29	D	Measurement & Data	Apply the area and perimeter formulas for rectangles in real world and mathematical problems.
30	B	Geometry	Identify perpendicular and parallel lines in two-dimensional figures.
31	B	Measurement & Data	Know relative sizes of measurement units within one system of units.
32	D	Number & Operations in Base Ten	Read and write multi-digit whole numbers using base-ten numerals, number names, and expanded form.
33	B	Number & Operations-Fractions	Use decimal notation for fractions with denominators 10 or 100.
34	A	Number & Operations in Base Ten	Read and write multi-digit whole numbers using base-ten numerals, number names, and expanded form.
35	C	Measurement & Data	Solve addition and subtraction problems to find unknown angles on a diagram.
36	D	Operations/Algebraic Thinking	Determine whether a given whole number in the range 1–100 is prime or composite.
37	D	Number & Operations in Base Ten	Use place value understanding to round multi-digit whole numbers to any place.
38	A	Number & Operations in Base Ten	Recognize that in a multi-digit whole number, a digit in one place represents ten times what it represents in the place to its right.
39	D	Measurement & Data	Measure angles in whole-number degrees using a protractor.
40	B	Measurement & Data	Use the four operations to solve word problems involving money.
41	D	Geometry	Identify perpendicular and parallel lines in two-dimensional figures.
42	C	Number & Operations-Fractions	Recognize and generate equivalent fractions.
43	B	Number & Operations-Fractions	Compare two decimals to hundredths by reasoning about their size.
44	B	Number & Operations-Fractions	Solve word problems involving multiplication of a fraction by a whole number.
45	D	Operations/Algebraic Thinking	Assess the reasonableness of answers using mental computation and estimation strategies including rounding.
46	D	Operations/Algebraic Thinking	Solve multistep word problems posed with whole numbers and having whole-number answers using the four operations.
47	D	Number & Operations in Base Ten	Fluently add and subtract multi-digit whole numbers using the standard algorithm.
48	C	Number & Operations in Base Ten	Multiply a whole number of up to four digits by a one-digit whole number.
49	A	Operations/Algebraic Thinking	Solve multistep word problems posed with whole numbers and having whole-number answers using the four operations.
50	A	Operations/Algebraic Thinking	Represent problems using equations with a letter standing for the unknown quantity.

Common Core Mathematics, Practice Test 1, Book 3

Question	Points	Topic	Common Core Learning Standard
51	2	Operations/Algebraic Thinking	Multiply or divide to solve word problems involving multiplicative comparison.
52	3	Number & Operations-Fractions	Understand, recognize, and generate equivalent fractions using visual fraction models, with attention to how the number and size of the parts differ even though the two fractions themselves are the same size.
53	2	Number & Operations-Fractions	Understand decimal notation for fractions, and compare decimal fractions.
54	2	Number & Operations-Fractions	Build fractions from unit fractions by applying and extending previous understandings of operations on whole numbers.
55	3	Operations/Algebraic Thinking	Generate a number or shape pattern that follows a given rule. Identify apparent features of the pattern that were not explicit in the rule itself.
56	3	Geometry	Recognize a line of symmetry for a two-dimensional figure as a line across the figure such that the figure can be folded along the line into matching parts.
57	2	Number & Operations in Base Ten	Read and write multi-digit whole numbers using base-ten numerals, number names, and expanded form.
58	2	Number & Operations in Base Ten	Multiply a whole number of up to four digits by a one-digit whole number using strategies based on place value and the properties of operations.
59	2	Measurement & Data	Apply the area and perimeter formulas for rectangles in real world and mathematical problems.
60	3	Geometry	Classify two-dimensional figures based on the presence or absence of parallel or perpendicular lines, or the presence or absence of angles of a specified size.

Q51.
35 hours
45 hours
40 hours
$270

Scoring Information
Give a total score out of 2.
Give a score of 0.5 for each correct answer.

Q52.
3 of 5 segments shaded
60 of 100 segments shaded
$\frac{3}{5}$ and $\frac{60}{100}$

Scoring Information
Give a total score out of 3.
Give a score of 1 for each correct shading.
Give a score of 0.5 for each correct fraction.

Q53.
The number 1.75 should be plotted on the number line.
Answer: $1\frac{3}{4}$ or $1\frac{75}{100}$

Scoring Information
Give a total score out of 2.
Give a score of 1 for the number correctly plotted.
Give a score of 1 for the correct answer.

Q54.
The model should be shaded as shown below.

Answer: $\frac{17}{10}$

Scoring Information
Give a total score out of 2.
Give a score of 1 for the correct shading.
Give a score of 1 for the correct answer.

Q55.
41

The student should identify that every number in the pattern will be odd. The explanation should show an understanding that every step involves adding an even number to an odd number.

Scoring Information
Give a total score out of 3.
Give a score of 1 for the correct answer.
Give a score of 1 for correctly identifying that every number will be odd.
Give a score out of 1 for the explanation.

Q56.
The isosceles triangle in the center should be identified as the shape that has a line of symmetry. A line of symmetry should be drawn on the triangle, as shown below.

 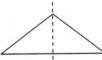

The student may describe how the two halves are the same size and shape or how the two halves can be folded onto each other.

Scoring Information
Give a total score out of 3.
Give a score of 1 for the correct shape identified.
Give a score of 1 for the line of symmetry drawn correctly.
Give a score out of 1 for the explanation.

Q57.

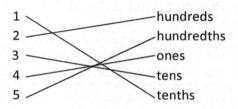

1 — tens
2 — hundredths
3 — hundreds
4 — ones
5 — tenths

$2 \times 100 + 3 \times 10 + 4 \times 1 + 1 \times \frac{1}{10} + 5 \times \frac{1}{100}$

Scoring Information
Give a total score out of 2.
Give a score of 1 for identifying place values correctly.
Give a score of 1 for writing the number in expanded form correctly.

Q58.
156

The work should show the calculation of 6 × 26 = 156.

Scoring Information
Give a total score out of 2.
Give a score of 1 for the correct answer.
Give a score out of 1 for the working.

Q59.
2,400 square feet

The work should show the calculation of 60 × 40 = 2,400.

Scoring Information
Give a total score out of 2.
Give a score of 1 for the correct answer.
Give a score out of 1 for the working.

Q60.
The column for 1 or more right angles should list A, C, and D.
The column for 1 or more pairs of parallel sides should list A, D, E, and F.
The column for 1 or more pairs of perpendicular sides should list A, C, and D.

Scoring Information
Give a total score out of 3.
Give a score of 1 for each column correctly completed.

Common Core Mathematics, Practice Test 2, Book 1

Question	Answer	Topic	Common Core Learning Standard
1	B	Measurement & Data	Use the four operations to solve word problems involving intervals of time.
2	B	Operations/Algebraic Thinking	Solve multistep word problems posed with whole numbers and having whole-number answers using the four operations, including problems in which remainders must be interpreted.
3	D	Operations/Algebraic Thinking	Find all factor pairs for a whole number in the range 1–100. / Determine whether a given whole number in the range 1–100 is prime or composite.
4	A	Operations/Algebraic Thinking	Represent problems using equations with a letter standing for the unknown quantity.
5	C	Number & Operations-Fractions	Understand addition and subtraction of fractions as joining and separating parts referring to the same whole.
6	B	Operations/Algebraic Thinking	Find all factor pairs for a whole number in the range 1–100.
7	B	Operations/Algebraic Thinking	Assess the reasonableness of answers using mental computation and estimation strategies including rounding.
8	A	Operations/Algebraic Thinking	Solve multistep word problems posed with whole numbers and having whole-number answers using the four operations.
9	C	Measurement & Data	Use the four operations to solve word problems involving money.
10	C	Measurement & Data	Know relative sizes of measurement units within one system of units.
11	D	Operations/Algebraic Thinking	Find all factor pairs for a whole number in the range 1–100. / Determine whether a given whole number in the range 1–100 is prime or composite.
12	C	Operations/Algebraic Thinking	Generate and analyze patterns.
13	D	Number & Operations in Base Ten	Recognize that in a multi-digit whole number, a digit in one place represents ten times what it represents in the place to its right.
14	C	Measurement & Data	Solve problems by using information presented in line plots.
15	D	Number & Operations-Fractions	Understand, recognize, and generate equivalent fractions using visual fraction models, with attention to how the number and size of the parts differ even though the two fractions themselves are the same size.
16	C	Number & Operations-Fractions	Use decimal notation for fractions with denominators 10 or 100.
17	A	Number & Operations-Fractions	Record the results of comparisons with symbols >, =, or <, and justify the conclusions, e.g., by using a visual fraction model.
18	C	Operations/Algebraic Thinking	Assess the reasonableness of answers using mental computation and estimation strategies including rounding.
19	B	Measurement & Data	Within a single system of measurement, express measurements in a larger unit in terms of a smaller unit.

20	B	Measurement & Data	Solve addition and subtraction problems to find unknown angles on a diagram in real world and mathematical problems.
21	A	Operations/Algebraic Thinking	Generate and analyze patterns.
22	A	Number & Operations-Fractions	Use decimal notation for fractions with denominators 10 or 100.
23	C	Geometry	Identify perpendicular and parallel lines in two-dimensional figures.
24	A	Geometry	Identify line-symmetric figures and draw lines of symmetry.
25	D	Operations/Algebraic Thinking	Represent verbal statements of multiplicative comparisons as multiplication equations.

Common Core Mathematics, Practice Test 2, Book 2

Question	Answer	Topic	Common Core Learning Standard
26	A	Geometry	Recognize right triangles as a category, and identify right triangles.
27	B	Number & Operations-Fractions	Decompose a fraction into a sum of fractions with the same denominator in more than one way, recording each decomposition by an equation.
28	D	Number & Operations in Base Ten	Compare two multi-digit numbers based on meanings of the digits in each place.
29	A	Number & Operations in Base Ten	Find whole-number quotients using strategies based on place value, the properties of operations, and/or the relationship between multiplication and division.
30	D	Measurement & Data	Know relative sizes of measurement units within one system of units.
31	D	Number & Operations-Fractions	Understand, recognize, and generate equivalent fractions using visual fraction models, with attention to how the number and size of the parts differ even though the two fractions themselves are the same size.
32	C	Operations/Algebraic Thinking	Generate and analyze patterns.
33	D	Number & Operations in Base Ten	Read and write multi-digit whole numbers using base-ten numerals, number names, and expanded form.
34	C	Measurement & Data	Represent measurement quantities using diagrams such as number line diagrams that feature a measurement scale.
35	C	Number & Operations in Base Ten	Recognize that in a multi-digit whole number, a digit in one place represents ten times what it represents in the place to its right.
36	B	Number & Operations-Fractions	Use decimal notation for fractions with denominators 10 or 100.
37	D	Measurement & Data	Use the four operations to solve word problems involving time.
38	C	Number & Operations-Fractions	Compare two decimals to hundredths by reasoning about their size.
39	D	Operations/Algebraic Thinking	Generate and analyze patterns.
40	C	Measurement & Data	Know relative sizes of measurement units within one system of units.
41	C	Measurement & Data	Use the four operations to solve word problems involving distances, including problems involving simple fractions or decimals.
42	B	Number & Operations-Fractions	Solve word problems involving multiplication of a fraction by a whole number.
43	C	Operations/Algebraic Thinking	Generate and analyze patterns.
44	A	Number & Operations in Base Ten	Find whole-number quotients using strategies based on place value, the properties of operations, and/or the relationship between multiplication and division.
45	A	Number & Operations in Base Ten	Read and write multi-digit whole numbers using base-ten numerals, number names, and expanded form.
46	B	Measurement & Data	Recognize angles as geometric shapes that are formed wherever two rays share a common endpoint.

47	B	Measurement & Data	Solve problems by using information presented in line plots.
48	A	Number & Operations in Base Ten	Recognize that in a multi-digit whole number, a digit in one place represents ten times what it represents in the place to its right.
49	B	Measurement & Data	Understand concepts of angle measurement, including that an angle is measured with reference to a circle with its center at the common endpoint of the rays, and that an angle that turns through 1/360 of a circle is called a "one-degree angle," and can be used to measure angles.
50	C	Measurement & Data	Within a single system of measurement, express measurements in a larger unit in terms of a smaller unit.

Common Core Mathematics, Practice Test 2, Book 3

Question	Points	Topic	Common Core Learning Standard
51	2	Number & Operations-Fractions	Compare two decimals to hundredths by reasoning about their size.
52	2	Number & Operations-Fractions	Use decimal notation for fractions with denominators 10 or 100.
53	3	Operations/Algebraic Thinking	Multiply or divide to solve word problems involving multiplicative comparison.
54	3	Measurement & Data	Sketch angles of specified measure.
55	3	Operations/Algebraic Thinking	Determine whether a given whole number in the range 1–100 is prime or composite.
56	3	Measurement & Data	Apply the area and perimeter formulas for rectangles in real world and mathematical problems.
57	2	Number & Operations-Fractions	Express a fraction with denominator 10 as an equivalent fraction with denominator 100, and use this technique to add two fractions with respective denominators 10 and 100.
58	2	Number & Operations-Fractions	Use decimal notation for fractions with denominators 10 or 100.
59	2	Measurement & Data	Use the four operations to solve word problems involving intervals of time, including problems involving simple fractions or decimals, and problems that require expressing measurements given in a larger unit in terms of a smaller unit.
60	2	Geometry	Classify two-dimensional figures based on the presence or absence of parallel or perpendicular lines, or the presence or absence of angles of a specified size.

Q51.
35.009, 35.061, 35.077, 35.101

Scoring Information
Give a total score out of 2.
Give a score of 0.5 for each number in the correct order.

Q52.
The numbers $3\frac{4}{5}$ and 3.8 should be circled.

Scoring Information
Give a total score out of 2.
Give a score of 1 for each number correctly circled.

Q53.
Part A
6

The work should show that 6 is the greatest number that divides evenly into 12, 18, and 24.

Part B
4

The work may show the calculation of 24 ÷ 6 = 4, or could use a diagram to represent 6 piles of 4 pennies each.

Scoring Information
Give a total score out of 3.
Give a score of 1 for the correct answer to Part A.
Give a score of 1 for the correct answer to Part B.
Give a score out of 1 for the working.

Q54.
The student should sketch a right angle equal to 90°, an acute angle of less than 90°, and an obtuse angle greater than 90°.

The explanation should show an understanding that the right angle must be 90°, while the other two angles do not have to be an exact measure.

Scoring Information
Give a total score out of 3.
Give a score of 0.5 for each angle correctly sketched.
Give a score of 0.5 for identifying that the right angle had to be exact.
Give a score out of 1 for the explanation.

Q55.
Prime: 23, 29
Composite: 21, 22, 24, 25, 26, 27, 28, 30

The student should explain that prime numbers can only be divided by themselves and 1, while composite numbers can be divided by at least one other number.

Scoring Information
Give a total score out of 3.
Give a score out of 2 for sorting the numbers correctly.
Give a score out of 1 for the explanation.

Q56.
Part A
240 feet

The work should show the calculation of 80 + 80 + 40 + 40 = 240 or (2 × 80) + (2 × 40) = 240.

Part B
80 yards

The work should show an understanding that there are 3 feet in 1 yard.
The work should show the calculation of 240 ÷ 3 = 80.

Scoring Information
Give a total score out of 3.
Give a score of 1 for the correct answer to Part A.
Give a score of 1 for the correct answer to Part B.
Give a score out of 1 for the working.

Q57.
The model should have a total of 47 squares shaded.
Answer: $\frac{47}{100}$

Scoring Information
Give a total score out of 2.
Give a score of 1 for the correct shading.
Give a score of 1 for the correct answer.

Q58.
0.7

The work may show dividing 70 by 100. The work could also show simplifying $\frac{70}{100}$ to $\frac{7}{10}$, and then writing the decimal 0.7.

Scoring Information
Give a total score out of 2.
Give a score of 1 for the correct answer.
Give a score out of 1 for the working.

Q59.
105 minutes

The work may show adding 60 minutes and 45 minutes. The work may also show calculating $1\frac{3}{4} \times 60$.

Scoring Information
Give a total score out of 2.
Give a score of 1 for the correct answer.
Give a score out of 1 for the working.

Q60.
The statements "2 pairs of parallel sides" and "4 congruent sides" should be circled.
square

Scoring Information
Give a total score out of 2.
Give a score of 0.5 for each correct statement circled. Take off 0.5 points if additional statements are circled.
Give a score of 1 for the correct answer of square.

CPSIA information can be obtained
at www.ICGtesting.com
Printed in the USA
BVOW09s0714260317
479466BV00005B/440/P